LifeTimes

The Story of Vincent van Gogh

by Clare Bevan
illustrated by Neil Reed

Thameside Press

US publication copyright © 2002 Thameside Press.
International copyright reserved in all countries.
No part of this book may be reproduced in any form
without written permission from the publisher.

Distributed in the United States by
Smart Apple Media
1980 Lookout Drive
North Mankato, MN 56003

Produced for Thameside Press by
White-Thomson Publishing Ltd
2/3 St Andrew's Place
Lewes, BN7 1UP, England.

© White-Thomson Publishing Limited 2002
Text copyright © Clare Bevan 2002
Illustrations copyright © Neil Reed 2002

ISBN 1-931983-16-X

Library of Congress Control Number 2002 141331

Editor: Kay Barnham
Designer: John Jamieson
Language consultant: Norah Granger, Senior Lecturer in
  Primary Education at the University of Brighton, England.
Art consultant: Felicity Allen, Head of Public Programs,
  Hayward Gallery, London.

Printed in China

Introduction

Vincent van Gogh was born in the Netherlands in 1853, the eldest son of a handsome preacher and his kind wife. Vincent loved the fresh air and the sunshine of the countryside around him. He watched the changing colors of the seasons, and filled his mind with pictures.

At sixteen, Vincent left home to work for an art dealer. But, although his job took him to Paris and London, he began to feel he was wasting his time. Maybe he should become a preacher, like his father. . . .

Prayers and Potatoes

"If you really want to become
a preacher, you must work harder at your Latin
and Greek," explained the teacher kindly. "If you
don't improve, you'll never pass your exams."

Vincent sighed. He did not enjoy his religious
studies, and he wasn't doing well. "But Jesus spoke
with deeds, not fine words," he argued. "I want
to be like Him, and devote my life to others."

The old man shook his head. "I know you mean
well," he said, "but you must follow our rules. You
must learn to study."

Vincent turned away. He was sure he was right. He didn't need to be a brilliant scholar to follow his dream.

Even when he failed his exams, Vincent was still determined to make his parents proud.

And at last he was given his chance.

Vincent was sent to preach in the mining villages of Belgium, where the people crawled underground like moles or rooted through the fields for potatoes.

No one worked harder than Vincent.
No one worked longer. He shared everything
he owned with the hungry families who toiled
in the dangerous darkness. He gave them his
food, his spare clothes, the last of his strength.

His hair grew wild, he looked like a
scarecrow, and he always seemed to be ill.

At home, his family grew worried.

"Poor Vincent," sighed his mother. "He tries
too hard. How can we save him from himself?"

"I'll write to him,"
said Theo, his brother.
"I'll remind him
how much he used to love the world
of pictures and the smell of fresh paint."

And Vincent did remember. Dragging
himself out of his pit of despair, he began
to draw and paint everything he saw.

And as he drew, he felt his strength
returning. I am not a preacher after all,
he thought. I am an artist.

Vincent had found his way—but it would
not be an easy path to tread.

Vincent stayed in a mining district called Borinage.
The miners were very poor and had to work hard just
to make enough money to eat. Women and children sifted
through the waste heaps for scraps of coal to heat their
homes, and often their main meal was a shared dish of hot
potatoes. Later, Vincent remembered those hungry times in
a dramatic picture called *The Potato Eaters*.

Tricks of the Trade

Vincent was determined to succeed as an artist.

"If I practice hard, I can become a great painter," he promised himself.

But before he could do this, he had to learn the tricks of the trade.

"I am using a perspective frame," he wrote to Theo. "It's a clever little gadget that helps me draw more accurately. Now I can show whether things are near or far away. And I'm taking lessons from Anton Mauve, the artist."

Over the next few years, Vincent sketched
the things he loved. The bony branches of
willow trees, black against a winter sky;
birds' nests woven from moss and grasses;
his hungry companions from the mining
village, eating their frugal meal of hot potatoes.

Steadily, his drawings improved, and he was
ready to learn more. It was time for him to
become an art student in Antwerp. "I will learn
from the painters of the past and create my
own masterpieces," he said confidently.

But as usual, nothing went as planned.

"Your paint is too thick," grumbled his teachers. "You hurry too much. And you don't follow our rules."

So they showed him how to work slowly, patiently, adding each tiny detail with a delicate brush. They showed him how to sketch statues of stone.

"There," they said to Vincent. "Lovely smooth surfaces. Lovely pale colors. That's what we want you to paint."

"But I want to paint *real* people!" protested Vincent. "I want to paint a fresh picture every day. I want to sit outside in the sunshine and paint the movement of the clouds, the sparkle of the water."

As soon as they were alone, his teachers groaned. "Vincent will never be an artist," they said. "We must move him to a lower group."

But they were too late. Vincent had already packed his bags and gone to stay with his brother Theo in Paris.

Since the discovery of perspective, hundreds of years earlier, many artists liked to use a perspective frame. Vincent's was made especially for him—he used it to see how objects lined up, and how he could make them appear closer or farther away. However, he felt quite proud of himself when he was able to paint landscapes without it.

Painting in Paris

For two exciting years, Vincent worked with some of the world's great painters. He met Georges Seurat and Henri de Toulouse-Lautrec, who were always ready to try new ideas. Here were people like himself, who wanted to capture this day, this moment.

"Now I can learn from living artists—who aren't afraid to break the rules," said Vincent.

He discovered the work of Japanese artists,
too—pictures with bold, simple shapes
outlined against clear backgrounds.

"I love their flowing lines and their strong
designs," Vincent murmured to himself.
"Somehow, I must find the money to buy
a collection for myself. . . ."

Now Vincent began to choose brighter, more cheerful colors for his own work. He painted windmills, and the bustling streets of Paris. He painted quickly and thickly, with fat brushes and flat knives.

"Who needs smooth surfaces and pale paint," he exclaimed, "when life is so full of glorious color!"

But soon it was time for Vincent to move on again. "You need a space of your own," he said to his brother, "and I need to spread my wings."

Seurat painted pictures made of tiny dots of color. Toulouse-Lautrec painted singers and dancers and designed wonderful posters. Both men belonged to a group of artists called the Impressionists. Like Vincent van Gogh, the Impressionists loved to paint swiftly, in the fresh air. At first, experts frowned on their pictures, but now they are among the most popular in the world.

Sunshine in Arles

Vincent was full of hope as he headed south for the French town of Arles. It was springtime, and the orchards were beginning to bloom.

He seized his brushes and worked from sunrise to sunset, overjoyed by the clear light and the gentle weather. "There are never enough hours in the day," he told his new friends. "I want to paint every tree, every branch, every blossom."

Vincent had brought his collection of Japanese pictures with him, and he painted the trees of Arles in the same flowing style. "I am pleased with these," he said to himself. "They are bold and bright and simple."

When Vincent heard that his old teacher Anton Mauve had died, he was sad. Then he thought of a way to show his feelings. "I will send one of my best pictures to his widow," Vincent whispered to himself. "My pink peach tree. It is just like a Japanese painting, and maybe one day it will make her rich."

Vincent's confidence grew
as he worked. He knew he
must constantly study and
practice, so whenever his
friends would let him, he
painted their portraits:
the postman; the soldier;
the dark-haired woman
who lived at the café.
And if they couldn't spare the time,
he could always paint himself!

As he squeezed bright coils of paint onto his palette, Vincent dreamed. "One day, I will set up a family of artists, here at Arles," he told Theo. "All my old friends from Paris will join me, and this will become my Studio of the South. We'll work together in the pure sunlight and inspire each other to create masterpieces. I can hardly wait to begin!"

Japanese art was very fashionable and popular. Rich people decorated their homes with Japanese ornaments, and Vincent loved his own collection of Japanese woodblock prints. He also liked to copy them, and many of them can be seen in the backgrounds of his own paintings.

The Sunflowers

In late summer, the sunflowers began to spread their golden petals. As they turned their heavy heads toward the sun, Vincent's eyes sparkled. He had an idea.

   "I am staying in a tall building I've called The Yellow House," he told Theo. "Paul Gauguin, the artist, is poor like myself. If I invite him to live with me, we can share the rent! Soon, more artists are bound to join us. Then more and more will come."

Bursting with excitement, Vincent began decorating his rooms. "Sunflowers!" he cried. "That's what I must paint. Yellow is the color of life and joy and energy. I will cover my walls with the flowers of happiness."

By day, Vincent painted huge bunches of blooms. By night, he painted the drowsy cafés of Arles. Indoors, harsh colors glowed under the whirling lamplight. Outside, the table tops reflected the shimmering light of the stars.

"Two thoughts are
always fighting inside my
mind,"Vincent wrote to Theo. "Sometimes
I want to scream and shout because I am so
poor. And sometimes I want to sing for joy,
because the world is so beautiful."

In his heart, he wished he could make
money with his pictures. Some of them were
used to pay his debts. Some were used to fill
his home with light. Others stood in stacks,
waiting, waiting, for the world to recognize
their greatness.

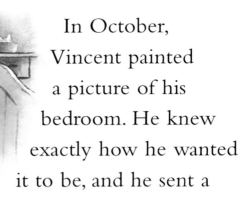

In October, Vincent painted a picture of his bedroom. He knew exactly how he wanted it to be, and he sent a sketch of it to his brother. "I'll make the whole scene restful and sleepy," he wrote. "The walls will be violet and the tiles red. The wood of the bed and the chairs will be as yellow as butter, and everything in my shuttered room will be as peaceful as a Japanese painting."

His house was ready to greet his friend Gauguin. His dream was about to come true.

When paint is used in thick brushstrokes, like paste, the style is called "impasto". This was Vincent's favorite method, because it gave his pictures depth and texture and a feeling of movement. Sometimes he used a palette knife, and sometimes he just squeezed the paint straight from the tube onto the canvas!

The Two Chairs

When Paul Gauguin arrived in Arles, Vincent was overjoyed. There was so much he wanted to show his friend—the night cafés, the Roman ruins, the green gardens. . . .

It was fall, and the days were growing darker. Vincent and Gauguin worked and talked until late at night, and at first everything went well. There were a few disagreements, of course, but that was only to be expected.

"Gauguin has painted a portrait of me," Vincent told his friends proudly. "He's used his imagination, and shown me with my sunflowers, but. . ." He frowned. "He seems to have made me look a bit crazy!"

Vincent remembered a picture he had seen long ago in London. It was an engraving of Charles Dickens's empty chair. Such a simple idea, yet it seemed to say so much.

"I will show the world how we are'" he said, "Gauguin and myself."

First he painted his own plain, wooden chair
with its seat of woven rushes. It was colored
a cheerful yellow, and beside it stood a box of
sprouting bulbs. Then he painted Gauguin's
elegant, red chair with its curved arms and
its books and its burning candle. Two very
different chairs for two very different men.

And things were not quite
right between them. The
disagreements turned
to arguments, and
the arguments
grew fiercer.

"You paint too roughly and too fast. You are much too fond of yellow," complained Gauguin, who was tired of the mess and the chaos in Vincent's rooms.

"You invent too much. You rely on your memory," shouted Vincent, who was tired of being criticized. "And you're much too fond of red."

"If that's how you feel, I might as well leave," growled Gauguin.

"No!" Vincent's heart thudded in his chest. "We are a team. What about my Studio of the South? You can't go!"

"Watch me!" And Gauguin
strode away, through the green gardens.

Vincent's world seemed to be falling
apart. "Everyone is leaving
me," he thought bitterly.
"Theo wants to get
married. Now I've
lost Gauguin, too.
Even my dreams
are fading away."

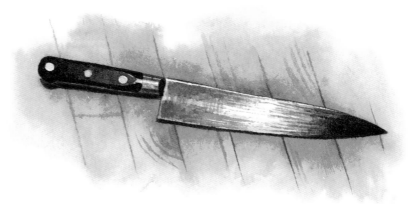

A knife glittered on the table, and he grabbed it like a weapon. "I'll make them all sorry!" Vincent cried. And in a fit of rage he started to hack at his own left ear.

By the time the postman found him, Vincent had pouring blood from his ear and had to be rushed to hospital. The Yellow House would never become his Studio of the South.

All his life, Vincent loved to read books, and one of his favorite writers was Charles Dickens. Stories like *David Copperfield* were full of action, but they also talked about uncomfortable subjects, like poverty. Vincent admired that, and when he saw *The Empty Chair* engraving by Luke Fildes, he bought a copy of his own.

The Hospital Garden

Theo rushed to his brother's bedside, and by January, Vincent had recovered enough to paint his own, brave portrait. This painting can still be seen today, Vincent looking calm while the white bandage reminds art lovers of his pain.

He was painting sunflowers again, too— crowds of blooms. But some of the people of Arles were afraid of him now.

"He is a crazy man who cuts himself with knives," they said. "Whom will he attack next?" So Vincent went to stay at the nearby hospital of Saint-Rémy.

At first, the place filled Vincent with horror. The other patients had blank faces and lifeless hands. It was as if they had nothing to do all day except stare into their own sadness.

But Vincent was never a man to sit still for long. He found friends among the doctors and peace in the woods and leafy gardens. In no time, he was painting again—vibrant pictures of blue irises, crooked olive trees, and tall cypresses like spiraling green flames.

"I think Vincent needs something beautiful to inspire him," Theo told his new wife, Johanna. "I'll send him some copies of his favorite pictures. He likes Gustave Doré's black-and-white engravings and Millet's paintings of people working in the fields."

When the package arrived, Vincent was thrilled. "I'll paint my own versions," he told himself. "But I'll give them movement and texture—and color! So much color!"

Inside the gloomy walls of the hospital,
Vincent brought life to other men's paintings,
and created new works of his own as well.
"For years, I have wanted to paint a midnight
sky," he murmured as he stood in the hospital
garden. "Now I have the paints I need, and the
time, too."

Filled with enthusiasm, he began to paint—
and he did not stop until *The Starry Night* was
finished.

Vincent put down his brushes and smiled. His picture was wild and exciting with its swirling lights and its towering trees. Beneath the sky were country houses and a church steeple that reminded him of his childhood home in the Netherlands.

Maybe one day soon, he would escape the prison of his illness and find freedom again in the outside world.

Vincent loved to copy the work of artists he admired. He liked Millet's paintings, because the people always looked so proud and dignified, even though they were poor. And he liked Doré's pictures because they showed unusual subjects—prison cells and dirty London streets instead of fine buildings and beautiful scenery.

A Taste of Triumph

"Vincent! You'll never guess what has happened!" Theo was bursting with joy for his brother. He had traveled to Saint-Rémy to see Vincent. "A man called Albert Aurier has seen some of your pictures. He thinks they're wonderful, and he's written a marvelous review! You see! You're going to be famous!"

Vincent nodded. "He's probably just being kind. There were much better paintings than mine in the gallery."

Still, it was good news at last—and there was more to come. Just a few weeks later, Theo became a father.

"My dear Johanna has had a little boy," Theo wrote to his brother. "And they are both well!"

Once, Vincent had feared that Johanna
would come between himself and Theo,
but she was an unusual person, full of warmth
and understanding. She and Theo had chosen a
name for the baby—Vincent.

Vincent was delighted. "This is a wish come
true," he wrote to his brother. "I just hope my
little nephew will always be happy. Please tell
dear Jo to take care and eat well."

Vincent himself was ill again, but in March the best thing of all happened.

"I have sold one of your paintings!" wrote Theo joyfully. "It's *The Red Vineyard* that you painted in Arles. You'll be a rich man very soon."

Vincent began to feel better. In May, he was well enough to leave the hospital. At once, he hurried to Paris to see his baby nephew.

"Vincent!" cried Jo with delight. "You look so healthy and strong! Stronger than Theo." But, as Vincent walked around his brother's house, he blinked with surprise.

Everywhere he looked, he saw his own paintings. *The Potato Eaters, Landscape from Arles,* and *Blossoming Orchards* decorated the walls. More pictures were stacked under the beds and behind the furniture. Jo had made her brother-in-law feel truly at home.

All the same, after three days Vincent was
ready to leave the crowded house. He must
find his own way—and now it led him north,
to the little town of Auvers-sur-Oise, where
there lived a friendly doctor called Paul Gachet.
He would cure him.

Some people say that Vincent only sold one painting during
his lifetime, but Theo probably sold others too. An uncle
bought 12 sketches of The Hague, and Vincent often used
his pictures to pay his debts! But without Theo's generous
gifts of money, Vincent could not have managed at all.

Wheatfields with Crows

What was wrong with Vincent? Maybe he had simply worn himself out. Maybe he was suffering from a disease like epilepsy—a disease that could strike like a thunderbolt and vanish as swiftly as a summer rainstorm.

No one can say for sure. But he worked harder than ever in his new home. "I am painting a new picture every day," he told Theo. "I can't bear to waste a single moment. Dr. Gachet is like a father to me.

He admires my work, and he even wants me to paint his portrait. I will make him look kind and thoughtful, and ask him to wear his favorite cap."

When Theo and Jo visited Auvers with their
son, Vincent met them at the station carrying
a precious present. "Here!" he cried. "It's a bird's
nest for my favorite nephew." And he carried
little Vincent around Dr. Gachet's garden, until
a fierce rooster made
the boy cry.

Then things began to slide out of control again. "My mind is spinning!" he wrote to Theo and Jo. "Please come and see me soon." But they were busy, and Theo was sick, too.

"Then I must work harder than ever," Vincent told himself. "I must fill every empty moment." So he sat outside whenever he could, painting the wheatfields of Auvers.

"The skies here are gray," Vincent wrote to his family. He missed the sunshine and the clear light of Arles, and his sadness grew like the clouds. Even when he painted the local church, his colors were dark and gloomy.

Finally, he could take no more. He staggered through the town to a wide cornfield, where he shot himself in the stomach. He did not die at once. He was carried to his bedroom and lay there for two terrible days. He died in Theo's arms, and a last letter was found in his clothes.

"Well," he had written, "I suppose I am risking my life for my work. . . ."

Vincent gave everything he had to his paintings, and one of his most famous pictures—*Wheatfield with Crows*—is also one of his last. The yellow grasses bend in the wind, and the dark wings swoop beneath a looming sky.

Vincent was only 37 when his life ended, and Theo died just six months later.

The two brothers are buried side by side, yet their names live on: in the loving stories Jo wrote about them; in the loving letters they wrote to each other; and most of all, in Vincent's dazzling and dramatic pictures that now hang in art galleries all around the world.

Many of Vincent's old friends came to his funeral, including artists from Paris who laid sunflowers on his grave.

The man who saw his pictures stacked under his brother's bed is now one of the world's best-loved artists; his once unwanted paintings sell for millions of dollars. Art galleries around the world are illuminated by his vision and by his joyful sunflowers.

Vincent van Gogh's Legacy

After Vincent's death, Jo looked after his letters and his pictures. She was sure the world would one day recognize his greatness—and she was right. At the beginning of the twentieth century, Vincent's name became famous, and at last his paintings were seen as masterpieces.

As time went by, Vincent's work was studied in schools and universities. His extraordinary life was dramatized for the theater, movies, and television. His genius was even celebrated in a song called *Vincent,* by Don McLean.

Today, his work is still loved, and his pictures are sold for millions of dollars. The greatest collection of his paintings can be seen at the Van Gogh Museum in Amsterdam. *The Yellow Chair* is in London's National Gallery.

You can also find copies of his pictures in art galleries and gift shops everywhere. Perhaps most popular of all are his joyful sunflowers, painted when he was full of hope in the Yellow House at Arles.

Timeline

1853	March 30	Vincent is born in Groot Zundert in the Netherlands, to Theodorus van Gogh and Anna Cornelia Carbentus.
1857	May 1	Theo van Gogh is born.
1869		Vincent begins work at Goupil & Sons, art dealers in The Hague in the Netherlands.
1872		Vincent's letters to Theo begin.
1873		Vincent is sent to work in London.
1876		Leaves Goupil & Sons.
1877		Studies religion in Amsterdam.
1878		Travels to Borinage in Belgium to preach.
1880		Begins to paint.
1885		Paints *The Potato Eaters*.
1886	January	Briefly studies art in Antwerp.
	February	Vincent goes to Paris to stay with Theo, who takes him to exhibitions of Impressionists' work.
1888	February	Vincent travels to Arles.
	September	Moves to the Yellow House.
	October	Paul Gauguin stays with Vincent.
	December	Vincent and Gauguin quarrel. Vincent wounds his own ear.
1889		Vincent finishes one of his most famous sunflower paintings.
	April	Theo marries Johanna Bonger.
	June	Vincent moves to the hospital at Saint-Rémy. Paints *The Starry Night*.
1888	January	Vincent's paintings are praised by Albert Aurier.
	January 31	Theo and Johanna's son is born. He is called Vincent.
1890		Theo sells *The Red Vineyard* to Anna Boch.
	May	Vincent leaves the hospital and visits Theo and Jo in Paris.
	May 21	Vincent arrives in Auvers-sur-Oise. Paints more than 70 pictures, including *Wheatfield with Crows*.
	July 27	Vincent shoots himself.
	July 29	Dies in Theo's arms.
1891	25 January	Theo van Gogh dies.

More information

Books to read

Camille and the Sunflowers by Laurence Anholt (Barrons, 1995)
Katie and the Sunflowers by James Mayhew (Orchard Books, 2001)
Eyewitness: Van Gogh by Bruce Bernard (Dorling Kindersley, 1999)

Websites

http://www.artchive.com/artchive/
   V/vangogh.html
http://www.vangoghmuseum.nl
Places to go

Van Gogh's paintings can be seen in galleries around the world. Here are just a few:

Museum of Modern Art, New York.
The Starry Night (1889)

The National Gallery, London.
The Yellow Chair (1888)

The Van Gogh Museum, Amsterdam.
The Potato Eaters (1885)
The Artist's Bedroom (1888)
Wheatfield with Crows (1890)

Glossary

canvas A strong material that can be stretched over a frame and used as a surface for paintings.
engravings Pictures cut into metal and printed with ink.
impasto Thick brushstrokes, used to create texture and movement.
Impressionists A group of artists who painted in a certain style.

palette The flat board used by artists to mix small quantities of paint.
palette knife A knife with a flat, blunt blade for spreading and mixing paint.
perspective The art of making things seem near or far away.
The Hague A very important city in the Netherlands. The Dutch government is based here.

Index

Arles	15, 16, 18, 20, 23, 29, 37, 38, 43, 46, 47	*Potato Eaters, The*	7, 38, 47
Auvers-sur-Oise	39, 41, 42, 47	*Red Vineyard, The*	37, 47
Gaugin, Paul	19, 22-27, 47	*Starry Night, The*	32, 47
		sunflowers	19, 20, 24, 29, 45, 46, 47
Impressionists	14, 47		
Netherlands, the	3, 33, 47	*Wheatfield with Crows*	44, 47
Paris	3, 11, 12, 14, 18, 37, 45, 47	Yellow House, the	19, 28, 46, 47